Thoughts from the Dark

Jenn D Lauren

BookLeaf Publishing

Jenn D Lauren

Presentation by *BookLeaf Publishing*

Web: www.bookleafpub.com

E-mail: info@bookleafpub.com

ISBN : 9789357447317

First edition 2022

ACKNOWLEDGEMENT

Thank you to anyone and everyone who has ever encouraged me to write.

Traveller

I have travelled many miles in these shoes,
Through chasms and plateaus,
All through the barren west,
But nothing there,
Interested me at all,
And as I walked, I felt,
This strange ache within my heart.

Far away, down the long winding path,
Beyond perilous journeys, and long sought
quests,
Past towering trees and crawling rivers,
I travelled and searched for what I was missing.

As I travelled, I met many strangers,
Tall and short, dark and fair,
They taught me to dance, to sing, and laugh,
But that was not,
What I had travelled for.
The ache in my heart, a thudding drum,
Is thundering in my ears.

The further I travelled, the more I learned,
I was searching, seeking, investigating,
For something I felt, not saw,
But all I wanted,

Was to belong to you.
That thought, that realisation,
Made my heart feel so heavy.

Like Tolkien and Lewis,
I've travelled afar,
Explored realm after realm,
Now, it's time to come back.
I'm being called,
Summoned,
Brought home,
By the wind at my back,
By the ache in my heart,
Driving me on, on,
And on…

The strangers travelled home with me,
Dancing and singing and laughing,
How many things,
Separated me from you?
I was counting the steps,
To get back to you as we went,
Over dusty paths and crackling rock,
Through shrubs and swamps and trickling streams,
And with each step,
My heart felt lighter and lighter still,
As I recognised all the paths that were leading me home.

Home,
Where I had left you,
And there I found you,
You were not waiting,
You were not wanting,
You were just – there,
When I needed it,
When I thought I didn't,
When I wanted it,
When I thought I didn't,
You were just – there,

These old, worn shoes won't last much longer now,
Covered in dust and dirt,
And their soles splitting and cracked,
But I have no need of them,
I don't need to travel,
To know what I,
Was travelling to discover,

But now I am home,
Now I can rest,
My feet may be aching,
My soul may be weary,
My head may be full,
But my heart is light with the knowledge,
The thought,

Though maybe it isn't much, this feeling of knowing,
But it is all I need,
Seeing you here,
To know I am not alone.

House of Cards

Yours is a house of cards,
I watched you build it,
Precariously balancing every piece,

You believe that it will stand;
A monument, a testament
To weather any storm,

But how can you be so sure?
Though it seems so stable now,
I wonder what gust of wind will bring it down?

Crashing on your head,
Those cards will slice your skin,
One stinging cut for each of the lies you've told.

Cataclysm

The heat is rising, the fire grows.
Where the path leads, no one knows,
In the darkness a flash of red,
But I am here and I won't leave you tonight.

Strangers come, darkness follows,
Parading soldiers strut over borders,
Whose hatred, what anger, drives them on?
No fear, no fear; I'm still here, I won't leave you tonight.

The dark night of broken glass,
Stripped of job, of duty, and of country,
Kicked out, chased out, expelled, removed,
Fined for the crimes of a roaming beast,
Chased away, I cannot stay; I want to be with you tonight.

Screaming voices, gunshots ring,
Fires lit and no one sings,
Backs breaking, bones creaking,
Buried to be forgotten,
And no one's brave enough to save you tonight.

Bloody skin and shaven hair,
Lost in darkness, the hope has gone,

The sun blocked out by ashy snow,
A proud star turned to ash,
And no one's here to save you tonight.

Families lost, your homes are gone,
The storm has come and now the sun,
Hope returns and so can I,
I won't leave you tonight.

Not now, not ever again,
I won't leave you alone tonight.

Hidden Beast

There is something crawling upon the skin,
Looking for an entrance, to get deep within,
It will make a home,
Multiply,
Then leave us rasping, withered and thin,

This beast we cannot see, burrowing in,
It will not let us be; when did this begin?
It's destruction is unrelenting,
Clamouring,
Though we're fighting, feuding within the din,

How do we escape this untold sin?

What can we do to earn some reprieve?
This thing has taken over,
Volatile, hostile,
We try to scream but our lungs are too weak to breathe,

This creature has taken hold within,
There is no escape from herein,
Drawing in, breathing in,
Gasping,
With one last breath, we let it win.

Dark Clouds

Warm sun, cool breeze,
A good day,
But storms creep on unsuspecting towns.

Home from school, all alone,
Eating snacks, knowing mother's home soon,

Thunder crashes, blinding light;
Wait for the rain.

Sun has set, howling wind,
A busy day,
But trouble creeps on unsuspecting homes.

Bundle into the car, all alone,
Pouring rain; finally headed home.

Dark clouds, cold night,
Jumping shadows, hearts race,
Don't fear, there's no one here.

Roaring winds, rushing cars,
Black bugs scuttle home,
Desperate to escape the incoming flood,

Thunder crashes, blinding light;

Wait for the scream.

Skidding tires, twisted legs,
Screeching horns and shattered glass,

Shooting pain, silence reigns,
Broken shell, shattered heart.

Siren rings, flashing light;
Waiting.

Still waiting…

Home alone, your body's numb,
Crippling fear in your eyes,
Crawl inside your big warm bed,
Hold yourself, your mother's dead.

Cleaning

Cleaning out my wardrobe, of all the things that
remind me of you,
All the memories you left behind haunt me now,
And it feels like you've barely left the room;
I swear I just saw you hovering by the door,
I hate to admit it, even to myself,
That even when I'm aching to move on,
All it would take is just one word from you,
And I'd drag myself back through all the pain,
Even though I'll deny it if you ever ask,
Ever question what I feel for you,
Because I am cleaning,
I'm cleaning out my heart, of all the things that
remind me of you.

Out of it All

Someone turn the lights on,
Let me find my way home,
Or at least some place,
That won't have me dying,

I'm begging,

For all the arguments,
I never began,
For all those words,
I left unsaid,

Out of fear,

Life's too short for caring,
And for you to see me;
I'm running away.
I need to move on now,

Out of pain,

If I could find a way,
If I could fix it all,
Find out what my life,
Is supposed to be worth,

Out of hope,

I want to fix myself,
I can't fix anything else.
I'll find a fortune,
That I would want to share,

I'm shattered,

I'm losing my control;
Destroying every hope,
This is what you do;
Killing the life you made,

I'm desperate,

To find love in the place,
Where no one feels they belong,
I'm losing my mind,
But I'm not the only one.

Tormented,

Do not let this pain carry on,
One act and the floor would shatter.
More hubris than even I can bear,
That you cannot take,

From me.

This Place

I walk through halls of my own creation,
Smooth steel or rugged rock,
Great fields or dense forest,
Vast ocean or rippling creek,
Great expanses that grow and change,
On a whim, on a thought,
This is my burden and my blessing,

To play in this nothingness,
This darkness that I can push aside,
In the light of whatever I dare,
Deign to create,
To grow,

I build castles and palaces,
Elegant towers and fierce cities,
Strong knights and stronger princesses,
Incredible heroes and invincible beasts,
This is my pleasure and my poison.

Churning and changing,
Rolling beneath my feet,
All this space and all this time,
To fill,
Crawling, creeping, crashing,
In my head.

Release me,
Let me escape from here,
Let me rest my eyes to see something real,
A solid thing that I can touch and hold,
Let me feel real.

This is Real

Go to bed.
Crawl into your blankets and curl up into a tight, safe bundle.
Let it go;
All of the pressure and stress and pain you have been carrying,
Hear yourself sob and feel your ribs ache.
This is real.
You're alive.
Roll onto your back and look up to the roof,
Then rise and pull your knees up to your chin,
Hear the whimper that escapes your lips
Feel the hot tears on your cheeks.
This is real.
You're alive.
Remember every moment of this.
Don't forget the pain when the sun rises.
When happiness dawns and makes you bright and warm.
But it's not time for that yet,
Lay down, close your eyes, relax into the
Warmth and safety, and sleep.
Hear him call to you in your dreams and feel his arms around you.
You wish this was real.
And you're still alive.

I Have Been Called…

I have been called,
To the podium,
Of sin,
To delay,
To demand,
Nothing.

I have been called,
To ignore my heart,
My beliefs,
I am to be silenced,
Forever,

I have been called,
Once again,
And I feel alienated,
Alone,
I attempted to fight,
This little hole,
You've placed me in,

I have been called,
So you could spit on me,
Deny me my rights,
My lefts,
So you could tell me that,
All I think and thought,

I am wrong,

I have been called,
As in your eyes,
I am weak,
I am fruitless,
I have no way to defend myself.

I have been called,
To hear your sins laid out as my own,
To hear rage spurt forth,
The rage that should be mine,
For all the promises you have broken.

I have been called,
By you,
But I stand,
For me.
With every cutting word,
Wounds you expect to burn and bite,
I turn every weakness into strength,

I have been called,
To stand and face you,
And face you I will,
The consequences of your actions have a face,
Have a heart, have a soul,
We have rage,
I am what you make of me.

Door of Revelation

There is a door that was slammed closed.
All its mystery and wonder locked away,
As the bolt slid home.
A thousand, million discoveries hidden,
From curious, ingenious minds,
Waiting to crack open the unknown eggs,
And explore the hidden depths.

The closed door,
With its peeling paint and chipped wood,
The polished brass handle,
And squeaking hinges,
… Or at least, they might squeak,
If one dared to open it.

Would the latch be jammed?
Has the wood expanded in its frame so the top corner catches?
How hard would one need to pull to bring the door ajar?
How hard a fight are we willing to undertake to break into that sweet unknown?

Even still, though it may be troublesome,
For a moment,
What is beyond the door is far too tempting,

The endless possibilities of the unknown,
Of what is in store for us,
When we break through the door,
Beyond the known,
Next,
What a fantastic, all consuming love affair,
The exhilaration of ‘what can we learn next?’

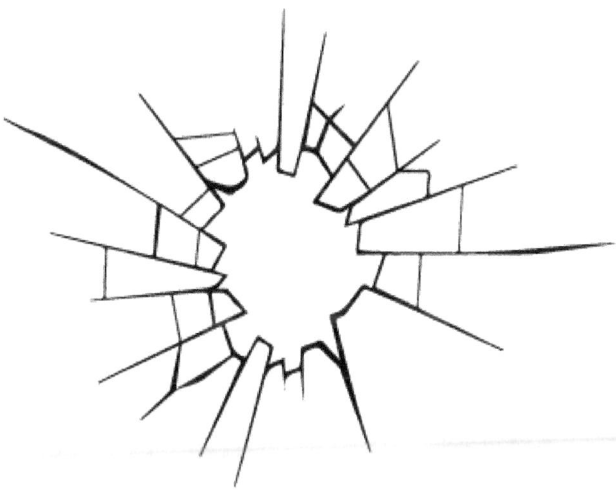

The Dream

I write down my dream,
I hide it away,
The memory fades,
But not the fear,

The scratching,
The claws,
The things I cannot evade,
Are breaking out from the seams,

Sewn up,
Again and again,
But still the stitches are cut free,
And the fear flows rich once again,

I wonder where it goes,
Once it’s released into the world,
Where do dreams go,
Once we wake up?

The dream,
The dream,
It tears me apart,
But I can’t remember,
How it came about.

Sometimes

Sometimes, it feels like any other day,
And then,
There's this sudden drop,
As if gravity has both given up,
And become immensely stronger;
Pulling your heart down,
While your stomach leaps and twists.

The person you love is no longer on this earth,
And they are impossible to reach.
For a moment,
The world ends again,
And you cannot imagine moving forward,
Now that person is gone,

How can you live while they do not?

You breathe slow,
Putting whatever pieces remain of you
Back together,
In some strange echo,
Of who you were before,

Then,
You move,
And you don't know how you can,

But you are,
And you feel brave,

So you keep going,
Day after day or hour after hour,
You always keep fighting the pain,
Because you know happiness still exists,

And grows,

And thrives,

Sometimes.

Scattered Thoughts - Scattered Mind

Pictures frozen in time,
Memories savoured and despised.
This world is ridiculous,
What is it really that you hold dear?
Just throw off your shoes and dance,
In maple syrup fever dreams,
Topped with ice cream and cherry pie.

And the words come to mind,
I just grab my pen to write,
But they're gone before I catch them,
On the paper.

Devil's traps and lightning scars,
A thousand cuts of a thousand miles,
But luckily the scars still fade,
As quickly as they are carved into pale flesh,
Even as this illness is settling into my bones,
Maybe even I can't shake it;

And the words race through my mind,
And I grab my pen to write,
They've disappeared before I catch them,
On the paper.

Never put your trust in a stranger,

Never have faith that the old dog changes,
It’s all the same mistakes,
With all the same reasons you left unsaid,
A thousand thoughts and a thousand choices,

A pen trembling in my hand,
I'm staring at a blank page,
I still have no words to write.
On. The. Paper.

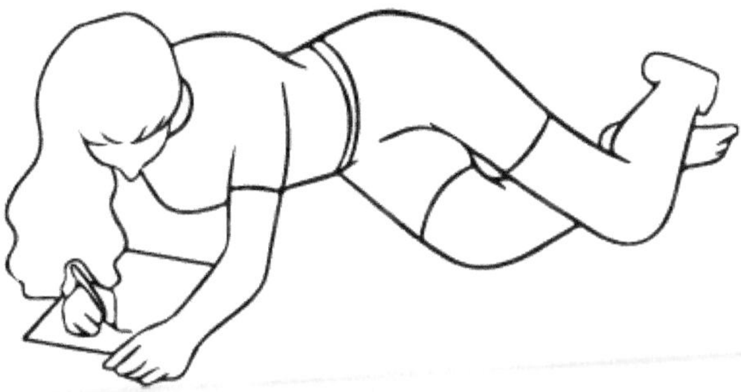

Little

Backed into a corner,
On a night the wind is howling,
When the Heavens are open,
Pouring,
And so is her heart,
She yells and she screams,
Cause she just can't hold it in anymore,

The rain is pouring down,
Like the tears on her cheeks,
As a car drives by,
She runs to the nearest house,
And bangs on the door,
But no one's home,
That house is as empty as her,

It's always 'just one little word',
And it's 'just one little thing',
But when those things come together
They're not so little anymore,

As a car pulls up,
And a boy runs out,
They're both so confused,
Girl and boy, staring blankly at one another,
For a moment that lasts an eternity,

Cause she's not his to love,
But he pulls her into his arms,
And he hugs her tight.

'Just one little word',
'Just one little thing',
But when those things come together
They are too hard to carry alone,

He's got her close,
There's nothing left to hide,
Cause she's gone far,
In so little time,
That tiny little smile,
As she looks at his face,
Is all he needs, to know,
She's going to be okay.

She's okay.

Crowded Little Street

On this crowded little street where we grew up,
Everything's swinging as the summer begins,
And there's nothing better than sittin' on the porch,
Watching the world go by,

But everyone goes mad as fire rains down,
And as the temperature rises,
School closes down,
And it's free to travel all around the state,

The crowded little street where we once lived is quiet,
Cause all the old men and all the old maids,
Lock themselves inside for that little icy breeze,
So the pretty young boys and curious young girls,
Go jump in the river to escape it all,

But everyone goes mad as fire rains down,
The temperature keeps climbing,
And it's hard to escape,
Four hundred fires burning all around the state,

The crowded little street where we grew up is roaring again,

I can't remember what it looked like at all,
As the fire rains down,
Covering my skin and dancing through my hair,
And as the walls come crashing down, falling in,
As the trees burn black and the ground's turned to ash,
That crowded little street seems mighty empty,
These dark streets aren't what we remember,

Chewed up by fire and spat out as ash,
Will you remember me?

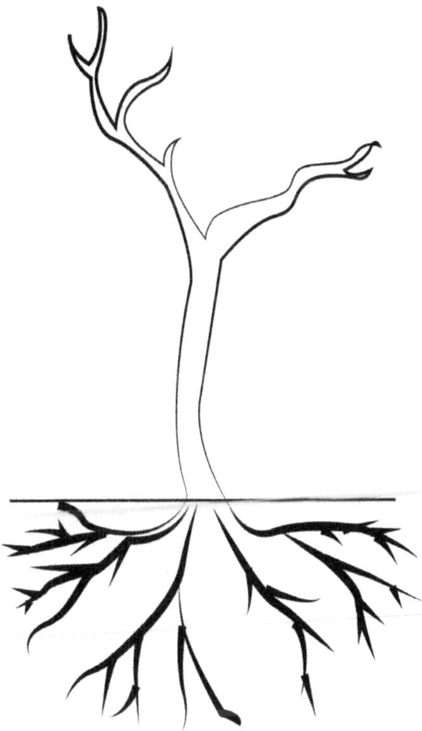

Phoenix

Hear the phoenix cry,
Answer the call.

Walk the halls and see the strangers of your past,
Feel their hearts beat, hear them scream,
Leave them behind in their graves,
Remember you're still alive,
Let yourself awaken.

Consumed in fire, left to burn,
Rise from the hearth, this is more than just a
birth,
Come back to life and learn to leave,
All the pain of your past behind,
Because it's time -

With a thousand shades of gold,
Lying in the ashes of sin,
The Phoenix's own cradle is it's parent's crypt,
Left in the Temple of the Sun,
Here's the place to be.

Hear the Phoenix cry,
Look to the horizon,
The sun will always rise,
Here's where we begin again.

When the world stops turning,
Falling away from beneath your feet,
Raise your head up,
Hear the Phoenix cry, calling you home,
A new day is dawning,
Here's where we begin again.

See the sun as it's rising,
Feel the warm of the sun,
Let it touch your pale skin.
Hear the phoenix cry,
Rise up.
It's time.

Sunset

If this was my last sunset,
Let me go peacefully,
Let me slip into a slumber where the angels of
my past welcome me.
Let me grow wings.
So that I could spread them in the sunrise of that
Next place and let them warm.
Let me soak up the heat of the sun and then soar.
Let me soar through the soft moisture of clouds.
Let me glide over fields and mountains and
rivers.
If this were to be my last sunset,
Let me see the ones I love.
Let me see their smiles and hear their laughter.
Let them hold me close.
Let me kiss their cheeks and see their eyes
Wrinkle and crease with joy.
Let this sunset be the best one.
Let all sunrises after be like a resounding call…
I am no longer here.
I have been called home,
But with a flash of green…
Every sunset, every sunrise,
I'll be soaring. I'll be watching.
Watching for the day you all hear the call to
spread your wings and fly.

Happiness

I'm done.
I'm finished with all the things that built up
Behind my eyes for weeks,
And months and years.
I want to be free and I will be,
Because I say I can be.
I'm through with waiting for things to change.
I'm going to make them change.
For better or worse,
Who cares when you're at the beginning?
It's the journey that counts the most,
And all those people who walk at your side,
Who make it all worthwhile.
It doesn't matter where my path may lead,
Because I'll carve it out of stone and metal,
I'll build roads and bridges just to get to where I want to be,
And when I arrive there,
I will dance and sing,
I will scream my happiness to the clouds and the stars and the great beyond.

But how long will it take me to learn –
That the place I want to be;
Is right here,
And it has been so all along.

I Promise I'll Always

A short sleep, a long drive,
I promise,
That no matter how little rest,
No matter how long the drive,
I promise that I'll be there.

Dark night, calling voices,
I promise,
I'll roll out of bed, pull you in close,
Let you sleep soundly,
Even when I cannot; I promise.

Confused faces, too many tears,
I promise,
No matter how angry or whatever we feel,
Or whatever was broken,
I promise I'll always bring you comfort,

Every award, all the accolades,
I promise,
All the achievements you gain, big and small,
I promise I'm always going to be proud,

Bruises or breaks, trips, falls and crashes,
I promise,
My arms will always be there,

To lift you up,
Through any pain and sorrow and heartbreak,
I promise I'll remind you how to smile.

All the time, all the distances,
They are all too much and nothing at all,
In the face of the love you have brought to me,

Of all these things,
Time, distance, love,
There will never be enough or too little to stop
me,
I promise to always love you,

Everything I am, I'd freely give,
Every piece of me I see in you,
Is a blinding light,
A piece of me you can have,
And hold,
Even when I'm not there,
A piece of me in you that calls me home,

Promising you, I'll always be here with you.

Shakespeare's Goodbye

Why does it take a minute to say hello and
forever to say goodbye?
I've never been one to say it,
But I guess the time has come,
For me to say what should never have to be said,
Even though I'm struggling to find words,
For all the things inside my head.

There's nothing that's done more for me,
Than what you've given me,
You've helped me trust myself.
Even though you might not notice it completely,
I know I've come a long way,
From the place that I began.

Though time may swallow us and leave us
wishing;
Wanting to go back to where it all started,
In all the years to come,
When you're watching strangers sit in the seats
that were once ours,
Remember that we don't need a place there,
For you to remember who we were.

Even though I could go on for twenty pages
more,

The most important thing I have to say is,
Thank you,
For all the things you've given me.

So now I guess it's time to say farewell,
"The elements be kind to thee, and make
Thy spirits all of comfort: fare thee well."

www.ingramcontent.com/pod-product-compliance
Lightning Source LLC
Chambersburg PA
CBHW051741130826
49812CB00033B/950
* 9 7 8 9 3 5 7 4 4 7 3 1 7 *